Quick and Fun Learning Activities for One-Year-Olds

Marla Pender McGhee

 **Teacher Created Materials, Inc.**

Cover Design by Larry Bauer

Made in U.S.A.

ISBN 1-55734-554-6

Order Number TCM 554

Table of Contents

Introduction

What a lot of changes a little person undergoes from twelve to twenty-four months! Happy one moment and frustrated the next, your one-year-old is in the process of becoming quite an independent little being. He is changing from an infant who needs you to do everything for him to a child who wants to do everything and say everything for himself even though he does not have the capabilities yet. You can generally expect the first few months and last few months of your child's second year of life to be a little more unsettling for both of you than the period in between, although there are great variations in normal development at this age. In fact, throughout childhood, children reach different development levels at different times.

How can you help this little person you love so much? Understand the frustrations of the desire to perform actions which he is not yet capable of; patiently demonstrate new skills; take the time to move at your child's pace; and be understanding of yourself as a human being who is not always perfect either. Remember that your child's mind is like a sponge at this age, taking in all that it can. Every idea he is exposed to is wonderful as long as it is not so advanced as to be frustrating.

Most important of all, remember to have fun as you play and learn together. Never again will your child be a one-year-old!

Author's Note

Due to a one-year-old's short attention span and easy distractibility, it is best to clear your work/play space of all items except those which are listed as materials for each activity. When a child is developmentally ready for a certain activity, it will hold her interest long enough for her to perform the activity at least a few times in a row. If a particular activity does not hold your child's interest after a couple of demonstrations, it may be a little too soon or a little too late, developmentally speaking, for your child to benefit from that particular activity.

Many of the activities in this book say that an adult should do something; however, an older sibling is certainly capable of facilitating many of these activities. Of course, all activities are meant to be closely supervised at this age, as safety must be of prime importance.

In addition to the activities listed in this book, twelve to twenty-four month-old children generally enjoy the following activities:

◆ toys representing real things so that they can imitate big people, for example, little brooms, play kitchens, toy cars

◆ building with large to medium-sized lightweight blocks

◆ simple wooden puzzles (Begin with those which have knobs on each piece, and then move to those which have one piece per space.)

◆ books with sturdy pages, bright pictures, and few words (Note the books listed in the Bibliography of Children's Books section at the end of this book.)

◆ any pounding or hammering toys

Last, remember that toys do not have to come from toy stores. As many examples in this book attest to, you can easily make items which will lead to *Quick and Fun Learning Activities for One-Year-Olds*.

Safety Concerns

Where your child is concerned, safety is of the utmost importance. The activities in this book have been designed with that in mind. Consider these saftey issues with your one-year-old.

◆ Your little one can climb. Keep poison, matches, and anything sharp locked up and out of reach. Do not leave his toys on counters where he will have to climb to reach them. He can and will. Also be aware that a curious one-year-old can climb through windows and open doors. Keep them shut and locked.

◆ A one-year-old is curious about everything. He will touch, taste, and smell anything, so take care in what you leave around. When you cook, keep pot handles turned into the stove so he cannot knock them off. If you leave loose change around, he may find it and put it into his mouth. If you are at the park or in the yard, check to see what he has in his hand. A creepy crawlie may easily wind up in his mouth.

◆ Keep outlets covered so he cannot put fingers or objects into the sockets.

◆ Check her toys. Are there any loose pieces? If the box says for ages three and up, it may have to do with the size of the toy parts rather than the fact that the child will find it fun. Explain to her that she cannot put anything into her mouth. Take it away if she does.

◆ Water play can present a whole new set of safety concerns. Never leave your child unattended while playing in or with water.

◆ Every so often take a tour of your one-year-old's environment from his vantage point. Are there sharp corners on a table that might need padding? Do you see cords that when pulled could easily topple a lamp? If you encounter such a situation, correct it now to avoid a possible accident later.

◆ Anytime you take your one-year-old in the car, even for just a quick trip, strap him into his car seat!

Stuff Around the House

Some of the activities in this book require a few simple materials. It is a good idea to collect the things you may need before you begin an activity. You do not want to frustrate your child and yourself when you begin something and find out you do not have what you need to finish the activity.

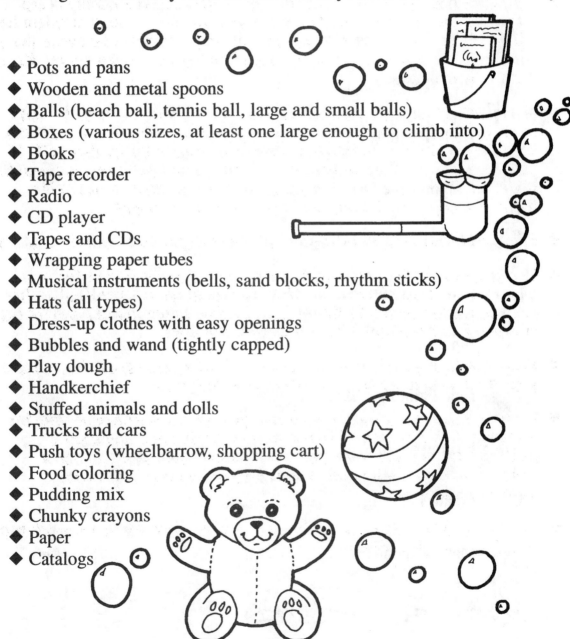

- ◆ Pots and pans
- ◆ Wooden and metal spoons
- ◆ Balls (beach ball, tennis ball, large and small balls)
- ◆ Boxes (various sizes, at least one large enough to climb into)
- ◆ Books
- ◆ Tape recorder
- ◆ Radio
- ◆ CD player
- ◆ Tapes and CDs
- ◆ Wrapping paper tubes
- ◆ Musical instruments (bells, sand blocks, rhythm sticks)
- ◆ Hats (all types)
- ◆ Dress-up clothes with easy openings
- ◆ Bubbles and wand (tightly capped)
- ◆ Play dough
- ◆ Handkerchief
- ◆ Stuffed animals and dolls
- ◆ Trucks and cars
- ◆ Push toys (wheelbarrow, shopping cart)
- ◆ Food coloring
- ◆ Pudding mix
- ◆ Chunky crayons
- ◆ Paper
- ◆ Catalogs

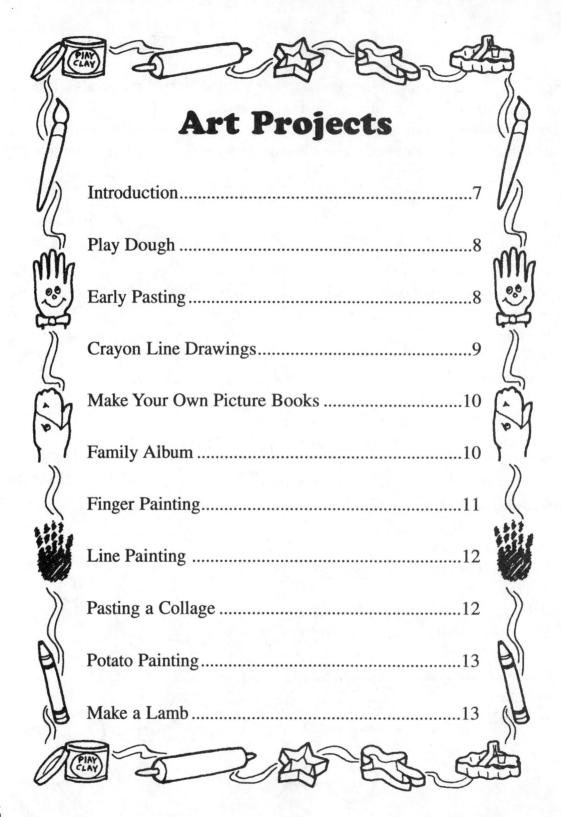

Art Projects

Introduction

Art projects at this age are about experimenting with and exploring new avenues of expression. They can be an invaluable tool for the child who is frustrated by not being able to express herself verbally. The art projects included in this book develop coordination in the large muscles of the arms and shoulders, which will be necessary for activities such as throwing balls. They help develop the small muscles of the wrists, hands, and fingers, which will be used to write as the child gets older. In addition to these physical benefits, the finished products your child creates will fill her with a sense of accomplishment. As she works through these new experiences, remember that art at this age is not about creating masterpieces but about the process itself. Undoubtedly, the finished products will seem like masterpieces anyway as they bring joy to you, your child, and other loved ones.

Note: A paint apron or old clothes for your child and a drop cloth for the floor or other work space are suggested for all of the activities in this section.

Play Dough

Materials

- Play dough
- Non-stick surface

Activity

For this activity, you can purchase non-toxic commercial play dough or make it yourself, using the directions provided below. Show your child how to pull or pinch off small pieces of play dough from the larger clump. Show him how to flatten it with his hands and how to squish it through his fingers. With older one-year-olds, demonstrate how to make a "snake" by rolling some play dough between the palm of one hand and the tabletop.

Homemade Play Dough

- 1 1/2 cups all-purpose flour
- 1/2 cup water
- 1/2 cup salt
- 2 tablespoons cooking oil
- a few drops of food coloring

Mix the ingredients well and store in an airtight container.

Early Pasting

Materials

- Old magazines or catalogs
- Construction paper
- Wax paper
- Paste
- Cotton swabs

Activity

First, place a little paste onto some wax paper and set it aside. Next, show your child how to tear pictures out of a magazine or catalog. Help your child to select colorful pictures. Show him how to paste by dipping one end of a cotton swab into the paste and rubbing or touching that paste-covered end onto the back of the picture. Turn the picture over and paste it onto the construction paper. Follow the same procedure with the other pictures your child has torn out, helping and encouraging him to do the pasting. Be sure that your child doesn't eat any paste.

Crayon Line Drawings

Materials

- Crayons
- Paper

Activity

As time goes by, your one-year-old will be able to imitate some specific crayon strokes instead of just scribbling at random. Be sure your child has had many opportunities to scribble randomly with crayons before attempting this activity. Additionally, this activity is better suited for older one-year-olds. Drawing horizontal and vertical lines begins to train the hands and eyes for future writing and reading. Just be sure that you draw vertical lines from top to bottom and horizontal lines from left to right, as you want to begin training the hands and eyes to move in the directions we use in reading and writing. Your child will switch from hand to hand as she draws, which is perfectly fine, as she is not yet ready to establish a dominant hand.

Sitting next to your child, place a piece of paper in front of each of you and then take one crayon in your hand and draw a few vertical lines from the top to the bottom of your paper. Give your child a crayon and encourage her to draw lines from the top to the bottom. If your child draws one or two lines as demonstrated but is then hesitant to draw more, encourage her by drawing more of these lines. Once this paper gets fairly full, or your child begins to lose interest, either turn the paper over or get another sheet and demonstrate how to draw horizontal lines from left to right. Encourage your child to draw horizontal lines across her paper, using the same method you used for encouraging earlier.

Make Your Own Picture Books

Materials

- Magazines
- Wax paper
- Cotton swabs
- Paste
- Zipper-lock plastic bags
- Construction paper
- Hole punch
- Two or three metal binding rings

Activity

Making your own picture books is a pleasure in itself, but in addition, it helps your little one create her own entertainment for later use. These sturdy books are also great in that they can be easily changed or added to. Pre-punch two or three holes just inside the edge opposite the zipper-lock end of each bag. Put a little paste onto a piece of wax paper. Help your child tear some pages out of a magazine. Then, demonstrate the pasting method introduced earlier in this section on page three. Be sure to paste pictures on both sides of the heavy paper. Place this paper into a bag and close the zipper-lock. This will help keep the pictures clean and nice. Help your child do the same with the other pictures and pages. Then, bind the book for your child by placing the metal rings through the holes and closing them securely.

Family Album

Materials

- Photographs
- Same materials as above

Activity

Put a little paste onto a piece of wax paper. As detailed in the previous activity, an adult should pre-punch one or two holes in the bags, depending upon the number of metal binding rings that will be used. Demonstrate how to paste one photograph onto each side of a piece of heavy paper and then insert the page into a bag and close the zipper-lock. When you have the desired number of pages, bind the book for your child by placing the metal rings through the holes and closing them securely. Then, enjoy his reaction to his very own book of loved ones!

Finger Painting

Materials

- Finger paint
- Construction paper
- Paint tray
- Easel
- Tape (optional)

Activity

First of all, if you are worried about a big mess inside, try finger painting outside. You may use commercially prepared non-toxic washable paint or make your own paint, using the directions below. Place one color of paint in the tray. (A shallow, plastic tray works best.) If using an easel, tape one piece of paper onto it. Show your child how to dip the fingers of one of her hands into the paint and then spread the paint from her fingers around on the paper. Also show her that she can make hand prints by dipping her hand, palm side down, into the paint tray and then pressing the hand onto the paper. Your child's work of art can be displayed or,used as wrapping paper.

Finger painting with pudding is not suggested for this age. It is best left until age four or five when the child has an understanding of what is and what is not to be eaten.

Recipe for Finger Paint

- 1 cup cornstarch
- 1 cup cold water
- 2 1/2 cups boiling water
- 1 cup non-toxic soap flakes
- a few drops of food coloring or vegetable dye

Dissolve the cornstarch in cold water. Add boiling water and stir well. Add soap flakes and mix well. Stir in food coloring or vegetable dye. Cool before using. Store in an airtight container.

Line Painting

Materials

- Non-toxic paint
- Large paintbrush
- Construction paper
- Tape
- Easel

Activity

To begin, tape one piece of paper to the easel. Using his brush, show your child how to lightly dip the brush into the paint, not getting too much on the brush. If your container permits, demonstrate how to wipe the brush on the inside edge to remove excess paint before putting the brush to the paper. Show your child how to paint a vertical line from the top to the bottom of the paper. (Children paint using their shoulders and elbows instead of their wrists and fingers at this age, so that is how you should move as you demonstrate this activity.) After showing him a couple of times, encourage your child to try on his own. If he is hesitant, try guiding his arm once or twice. If he still does not follow your example, just encourage him to make random strokes on the paper.

Pasting a Collage

Materials

- Collage bag
- Construction paper
- Paste
- Wax paper
- Cotton swabs

Activity

Give your child a piece of construction paper to be the foundation for his collage. Take one for yourself, too, as you will have more fun working together instead of being an observer. Empty the contents, or part of the contents, of the collage bag. Put a small amount of paste onto a piece of wax paper. Set cotton swabs nearby.

Demonstrate how to dip one end of a cotton swab into the paste and then pick up a piece of the collage material and dab the paste on the back. Now, place the material on the construction paper. Demonstrate this procedure with a few different pieces from the collage bag. Then, help and encourage your child to follow this procedure.

Potato Painting

Activity

Materials

- One potato
- Non-toxic paint
- Shallow container
- Thick paper

An adult should cut the potato in two so that each end can serve as a handle. Use two colors of paint, one for each potato half. Begin with one potato half and one color of paint in a shallow container. Show your child how to dip the cut end of the potato in the paint. Then, show her how to set it on the paper briefly, pick it back up, put it back in the paint, and repeat the whole process. After she has used this potato and color for a while, switch to the other potato half and another color. Praise your child's efforts as she makes this potato painting. Be sure your child wears a paint apron and that you use a drop cloth on the floor or table for this activity.

Make a Lamb

Activity

Materials

- Construction paper
- Cotton balls
- Paste

An adult should cut out of construction or other heavy paper, a very basic pattern for the lamb's body (an expanded stick figure animal will be fine). Then, show this to your child and say, "We are going to make a lamb. Lambs are soft animals." Let your child help you cover one side of the lamb's form with paste and then help your child cover the paste with cotton balls. Help your child clean her hands between steps if necessary. Diaper wipes are great for quick washing like this. Encourage your child to pat the lamb once the cotton balls have been put on, saying, "Feel the lamb. It's so soft." **Note:** This lamb is meant to be used with the "Night, Night Little Lamb" activity found in the "Music and Movement" section of this book.

Sensory-Motor Games

Introduction

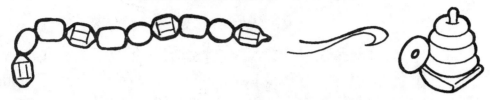

During the first two years of life, a child receives information about the world chiefly through his senses and motor activity. As the title implies, the games and activities in this section will help develop and refine your child's motor skills and senses.

Through these activities, your child will begin to develop the skill and knowledge bases which will be crucial to later physical and academic abilities.

These games and activities will appeal to your child's sense of wonder and will help him feel a sense of accomplishment as he develops new skills and realizes new abilities. At this age, every experience is new and exciting to your child; just remember that as he does these activities, he is also learning.

Squeezy Bottles

Materials

- Empty plastic bottles

Activity

Show your child how to hold one of the bottles under the water as it fills up and bubbles come out. Then show her how to pour the water back out into the tub. Encourage her to try this activity over and over using different bottles.

Where's Baby?

Materials

- Sturdy furniture

Activity

This exciting, spontaneous game is good, as are all forms of peek-a-boo, because they help your child understand that people or things which are temporarily out of sight still exist. This is the important concept of "object permanence" which helps make your child's world a more secure place as she begins to realize that mommy and daddy still exist even when they are out of sight.

Begin this game when your child naturally goes behind a piece of furniture as she walks or crawls around the room. Pretending you cannot see her and using a playful (rather than alarmed) tone of voice, say, "Where is _____?" (using your child's name). Repeat this question a few more times, if necessary, until your child emerges. When she does pop back out from behind the furniture, exclaim happily, "There's _____!" (using your child's name).

When your child is developmentally ready for this activity, she will repeat the hiding over and over (often in the exact same spot, which is fine) until you initiate another activity or she eventually tires of it.

Bean Bag Drop and Fetch

Materials

- Hand-held bean bags
- Basket

Activity

Sitting next to your child (on the floor is best), place the bean bags in a pile in front of you. Place the basket in front of you, next to the bean bags. Pick up one bean bag at a time and drop it in the basket. Then take all the bean bags back out, one at a time, and put them back in a pile. Move the basket and bean bags so they are directly in front of your child. By this time he will probably be reaching for the bean bags; if not, encourage him to do so. Help him follow the procedure you just demonstrated.

This game can also be played with tennis balls and clothespins. (It is best to use the clothespins that are constructed as one piece, since the ones with metal pins can pinch little fingers or come apart, yielding dangerous, small pieces.) Also, try soft, play balls and have your child stand while putting them in a basket.

X Can

Materials

- Large coffee can
- Round oatmeal box
- Small toys

Activity

Cut a large "X" in the center of the plastic can or box lid. Sit with your child, placing the X Can and the small objects in front of you. (Be sure to choose objects small enough to be pushed through the lid but too large to be swallowed.) Show her how to push the objects through the X and then how to take off the lid and retrieve them one at a time and place them in a pile together. Replace the lid. (You may need to help with removing and replacing the lid.) Move the can and objects in front of her so she can give it a try.

Pot Tops

Materials

- Pots and pans
- Lids

Activity

This is a great activity for your child to do right there in the kitchen with you while you cook dinner. In addition, it helps develop hand-eye coordination and the ability to estimate size. Just take a few minutes to demonstrate this activity to her before you start cooking and enjoy a little freedom to prepare dinner alongside your child's fun!

Take the pots and their lids out of your cabinet and place them on the floor or at a child-sized table. Sit down with your child and show her how to grasp the top of a lid and try it on different pots until it fits. (Do not immediately put it on the correct pot.)

Demonstrate this procedure until all the pots have the correct lids on them. Take the lids back off and then help your child put them on again.

Children enjoy it when a lid is too small and falls in with a crash. They will also initially think a lid that is too big fits a pot just because it does not fall in. All this is fine—as your child gets older she will begin to know when a lid actually fits and will then get the most pleasure out of finding the correct fit. Until then, expect some loud crashes followed by squeals of delight.

Nesting Cups

Materials

- Plastic measuring cups

Activity

Take out the 1 cup, 1/2 cup, and 1/4 cup measuring cups. (The 1/3 cup makes this activity more difficult, so add it in later.) Sitting with your child, demonstrate how to separate the cups and then how to put them back inside each other. Be sure to put the 1/2 cup inside the 1 cup and then the 1/4 cup inside the 1/2 cup, which is already inside the 1 cup, as this is the easiest way. Take the cups apart again. Help your child arrange the cups again.

Lock Board

Materials

- One thick piece of wood
- Easy-to-work latches or locks
- Screwdriver

Activity

This activity needs to be prepared in advance. Once made, it provides a great deal of stimulating, problem-solving opportunities for her. It is useful in developing your child's memory, as well as logical thinking and problem-solving skills.

Prior to working with your child, use a screwdriver to secure two or three simple latches to the board you have prepared. (A round, square, or rectangular piece of wood works best. Be sure to sand the corners or edges if necessary.)

Sitting on the floor with the lock board in front of you or in your lap, or sitting at a small table with the lock board on the table in front of you, demonstrate how to work the latches. Try each one a few times before demonstrating how to work the next one. After showing all the latches to your child, place the board in front of her and help her work the latches by herself.

19

Big and Little Can

Materials

- Large coffee can
- Plastic lid
- Various objects

Activity

This is a peek-a-boo activity which can be done before (as an introduction) or after (as reinforcement) your child begins understanding the concepts of big and little.

Cut one large and one small hole in the plastic coffee can lid. Sit with your child either on the floor or at a small table and place the can and all the objects in a pile in front of you. It is best to have a few objects that will fit through the smaller hole and a few for the bigger hole. Be sure that the smaller objects do not pose a choking hazard!

Demonstrate how to put the objects in the can one at a time, showing your child how to put each object through the smaller hole first and then if it does not fit, trying it in the larger hole. After all the objects have been put inside, take off the lid and put the objects into a pile in front of her. Put the lid back on and then move the can in front of her. Encourage her to follow the procedure you demonstrated. Once she has some success with this activity, encourage her to do it repeatedly. Do not worry if she puts some objects through the larger hole which really could have fit through the smaller hole. She will soon develop the skills to choose which option is better for each item.

Magic Tube

Materials

- Paper towel tube
- Small objects

Activity

This activity capitalizes on the fact that young children love to see something disappear and then reappear. Be sure the objects you use to slide through the tube are large enough to not pose a choking hazard for your child. Good examples include a spoon, comb, and baby sock.

Sitting on the floor with your child, place the small objects in front of you and hold the tube in your hand. Show your child how to put the objects, one at a time, into the tube with one hand, while holding the tube at a slight angle with the other hand. Then have her watch with you as the objects come out the other end.

After you have put all the objects through once, move the pile of objects in front of your child and hand her the tube. Help her continue the game and watch items disappear and then reappear.

If your child has a hard time holding the tube in the air and putting the objects into it at the same time, try having her hold the tube so that one end rests on the floor while she puts the objects inside. Then have her lift the tube to see where the objects have gone.

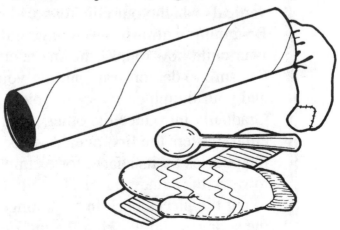

Button-Button

Materials

• One large button

Activity

Sit facing your child and hold out the palms of your hands. Then, take a button and point out to your child that you are putting the button in a certain hand. Close your hands briefly and say, "Where's the button?" Then, open them and say, "Look, there's the button." Show your child that you are switching hands and then repeat the same procedure as above. Do this, alternating hands, several times. At this age you should always show your child which hand the button is in before closing your hand and having him guess. As your child gets older, you can make this more challenging by hiding your hands behind your back and switching the button before having him guess.

Sponge Puzzles

Materials

• Four sponges

Activity

An adult should cut the following shapes out of each of the sponges: a circle, square, triangle, and rectangle. In the center of each sponge, cut a slit (horizontal or vertical) which your child can use in gripping the pieces. Beginning with just one sponge puzzle, demonstrate for your child how to take the shape out and put it back in. (Be sure to demonstrate putting your fingers in the slit and your thumb on top of the piece to move it in and out). Gradually introduce the other sponge puzzles as your child masters the first one. Also be sure to call each of the puzzles by its shape, for example, "Now we are going to work the square puzzle." If your child finds it difficult to put the pieces back in the sponges at first, try wetting the sponges and working the puzzles on a cookie sheet.

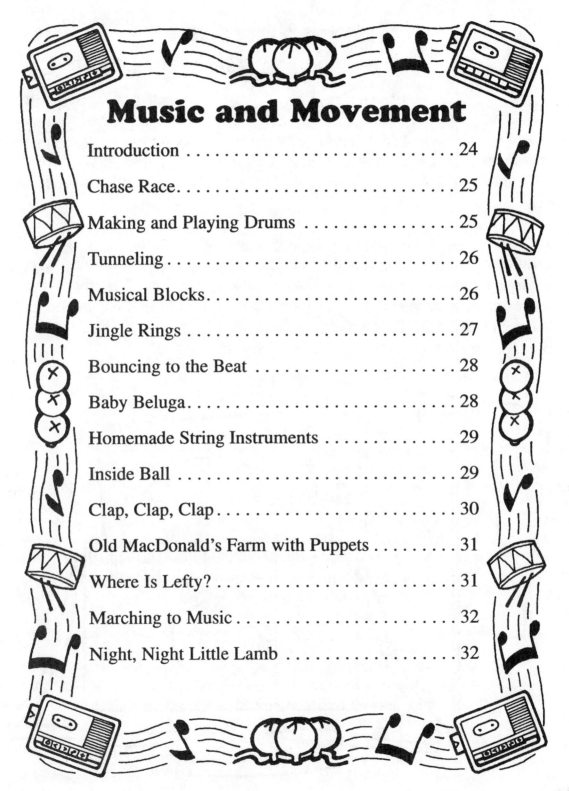

Music and Movement

Introduction

As soon as little ones can move, that is all they want to do. The more mobile they become, the more true this seems. One-year-olds just love to move!

The activities listed in this section help you take advantage of your child's natural desire to move constantly. The activities in this section help develop body image and awareness, as well as a sense of rhythm. The joy of discovering new avenues of expression is also inherent in these music and movement activities. Enjoy the many hours of fun to come. Keep the camera handy as your child entertains everyone around!

Chase Race

Activity

Materials

• None

As your child crawls or walks around the room, begin to follow him, saying in a playful voice things like, "Here I come. I'm going to catch you!" Some children like to be caught when playing chase, and others do not. Find out what your child prefers and honor his wishes.

When playing "Chase Race" with a walker, wait until he is good enough at walking to be steady on his feet. You may wish to crawl or walk on your knees when chasing a walker. Though this can be painful on your knees, try to crawl when chasing a crawler. Keep in mind, the cross-lateral movements of crawling are great for your child as they help to integrate the hemispheres of the brain.

Making and Playing Drums

Activity

Materials

• Coffee cans
• Coffee can lids
• Wooden spoon

Sitting on the floor with your child, place the cans and the wooden spoon in front of both of you. First, show your child how to tap the spoon on one of the drums by holding the handle and tapping the coffee can lid with the stirring end. Demonstrate this tapping procedure on all of your drums, gradually increasing the force of the tapping until it is more like pounding. Hand your child the wooden spoon and encourage her to imitate this drumming action. If she has a hard time making the spoon hit the lids of the drums, demonstrate how to tap and pound with your hands instead.

Tunneling

Materials

- Large cardboard boxes
- Heavy-duty tape

Activity

Open the ends of the boxes and tape them together along the outside edges, creating a tunnel. Be sure the boxes you use are large enough for you to crawl through, as you will need to demonstrate, and you may need to crawl in and help your child get out.

Once the boxes are taped together, encourage your child to crawl in first. Then follow and encourage him to crawl through the entire tunnel.

When you do this activity the first few times, make the tunnel straight. However, as your child becomes older and more independent, you may wish to make the tunnel turn a corner.

Musical Blocks

Materials

- Two blocks of wood
- Sandpaper
- Glue
- Marching music
- Cassette or CD player

Activity

Make the musical blocks by gluing one piece of sandpaper to cover one of the largest flat surfaces of each block. Wait until the glue has completely dried before attempting the rest of this activity.

Demonstrate this activity by holding one block in each hand with the sandpaper-covered sides facing away from your palms. Then slide the sandpaper-covered sides against each other to make a scratching sound. Give the blocks to your child and encourage her to do as you demonstrated. Once she has mastered this step, turn on some music and encourage her to keep playing the blocks. Sooner or later, you will find that she is playing the blocks in time to the music.

Jingle Rings

Materials

- Key rings
- Jingle bells
- Words to the song (See below.)

Activity

Secure the jingle bells (can be purchased at a craft store) by sliding them onto the key ring(s). With your child, hold one ring in your hand, or one in each hand. Show her how to shake the rings and make the bells jingle. Hand the ring(s) to your child and encourage her to shake them as you just did.

Once she has mastered this, teach her the words below. Then, sing together as she shakes the jingle rings.

As an alternative, your child may enjoy putting the jingle rings on her wrists or arms and dancing around as you sing the song together.

Revised words to Jingle Bells

(sing to traditional Jingle Bells tune)

Jingle Bells! Jingle Bells!

Jingle all the way!

Oh, what fun it is to jingle,

My jingle bells today!

Bouncing to the Beat

Materials

- Music
- Cassette or CD player

Activity

Start playing the music. Standing near your child, keep both feet on the floor and bounce up and down in time with the music. Encourage your child to join in the fun and do as you are doing. If your child has good balance, you may want to add some arm motions, as well.

Next time, try using different music selections with faster or slower beats.

Baby Beluga

Materials

- Recording of "Baby Beluga"*
- Plastic whale
- Blue food coloring
- Plastic container

Activity

Fill a plastic dish pan or other large plastic container half full of cool water and then add a few drops of blue food coloring to make the "deep blue sea." Show your child how to make the toy whale swim along and encourage him/her to do this while you both sing the song. She will quickly pick up on how to make the whale swim along, but will learn the song gradually, so be patient.

Note: If you can't find a plastic whale, a plastic fish will do. Later when your child is older you can explain that whales are not really fish.

*"Baby Beluga" by Raffi on Troubadour Records, 1982.

Homemade String Instruments

Materials

• Shoe box
• Rubber bands

Activity

Take the lid off the box and stretch each rubber band across the opening and underneath the box. Show your child the instrument and say, "We are going to make some music." Demonstrate how to use the thumb and forefinger to pluck the rubber band strings. Help her pluck the strings in this manner. After she masters this, show her how to strum the strings by turning her hand over with the fingers together and running her fingernails backwards across the strings.

Keep in mind that using rubber bands of different lengths and thicknesses will help vary the sounds your child can make with this instrument. Also, this string instrument should only be used under close adult supervision, as rubber bands could be removed and present a choking hazard if put into your child's mouth.

Inside Ball

Materials

• One ball

Activity

You and your child should sit on the floor, close to and facing each other, with your legs apart. Demonstrate how to push the ball with both hands so that it rolls to your child. Encourage him to push the ball with both of his hands so that it rolls back to you. Be sure to introduce the word "roll." Once your child has mastered rolling the ball like this, you can gradually move farther away from each other as you continue to play.

Clap, Clap, Clap

Materials

• Words to the song (See below.)

Activity

This is a body poem. Body poems increase awareness of the names and some of the functions of body parts.

Stand facing your child as you say and demonstrate the actions to "Clap, Clap, Clap." Encourage your child to join in on the actions and the words as you continue to repeat them.

Your child will most likely pick up the actions to this poem before he picks up the words. Over time, and with your help, he will learn more and more words.

"Clap, Clap, Clap"

Clap, clap, clap your hands, clap your hands together.

Clap, clap, clap your hands, clap your hands like me.

(Clap once each time you say "clap.")

Stomp, stomp, stomp your feet, stomp your feet together.

Stomp, stomp, stomp your feet, stomp your feet like me.

(Stomp your feet each time you say "stomp.")

Touch, touch, touch your knees, touch your knees together.

Touch, touch, touch your knees, touch your knees like me.

(Touch both knees with your palms each time you say "touch.")

Old MacDonald's Farm with Puppets

Materials

- Animal hand puppets
- Words to the song (See page 64.)

Activity

First show your child how to put on the hand puppets and demonstrate making the appropriate animal noise for each puppet as you sing "Old MacDonald Had a Farm." The first time through, whenever you get to the name of an animal, put that puppet on and move the puppet when you make its sound. The next time through, help your child put on the puppets and encourage her to sing.

Where Is Lefty?

Materials

- Words to the song (See below.)

Activity

Sitting on the floor next to your child, sing and act out "Where Is Lefty?" while he watches. The second time through, help him put out his left or right hand at the appropriate time and move them as directed.

Where Is Lefty?

Where is Lefty? Where is Lefty?

Here I am. (Put your left hand in front of your body.)

Here I am. (Wave your left hand back and forth.)

How are you today, friend? (Turn your left hand around to face yourself.)

Very well, I thank you. (Wave to yourself.)

Run away. Run away. (Hide your left hand behind your back.)

Marching to Music

Materials

- Marching music
- Cassette or CD player

Activity

Once your child is steady on her feet, she is ready to try marching. Once you integrate the arm movements, marching will include the same beneficial cross-lateral movements which are used in crawling.

Begin playing the marching music and demonstrate marching in place (high, bent-knee stepping at first; alternating arms can be added later). Encourage your child to imitate you so that you are both marching in place. Once your child has mastered marching in place, demonstrate marching around the room and encourage her to do the same.

Night, Night Little Lamb

Materials

- Stuffed lamb
- Words to song (See below.)

Activity

Have your child get a lamb stuffed animal. Then, tell her, "It's time for your lamb to go night, night." Tell your child that she can rock, hold or cuddle her lamb while you both sing a song. Help your child sing the song below. Night, Night Little Lamb (Sing to the tune of "Mary Had a Little Lamb.")

Night, Night Little Lamb

Night, Night Little Lamb, Little Lamb, Little Lamb.

Night, Night Little Lamb,

I really do love you.

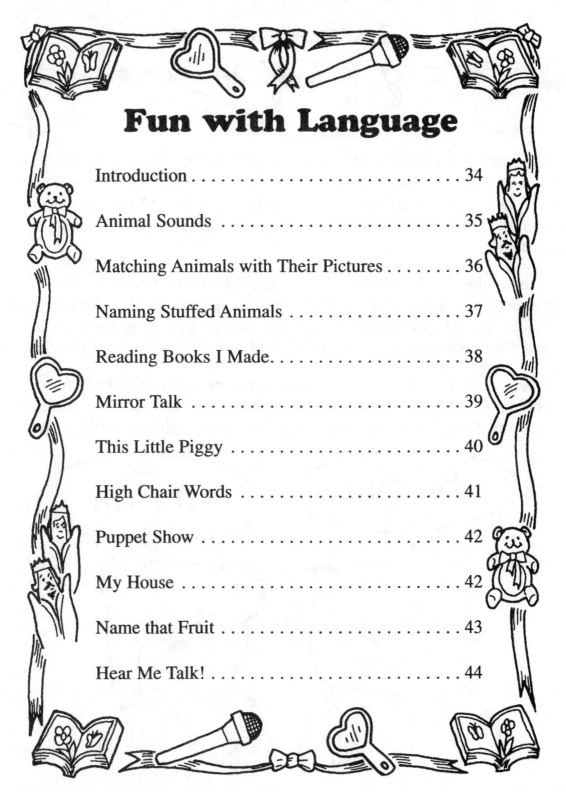

Fun with Language

Introduction

Language! It is one of the fundamental things that sets humans apart from other animals. It is also one of the things that sets toddlers apart from babies, as it marks a definite trend toward independence. For a toddler, learning to speak her native language is a very exciting, yet frustrating, process.

The activities in this section are designed to help build your child's vocabulary with words that are meaningful in her world. All of the activities in this book, and all of the other activities you participate in together, present wonderful opportunities for expanding and enriching your child's vocabulary.

Remember that your child can understand more words than she can speak. Do not be afraid to use a much larger vocabulary than your child currently uses in speaking, for this is the primary way her vocabulary will expand.

Animal Sounds

Materials

- Stuffed animals
- Pictures of animals

Activity

This activity introduces language in a stimulating way, with animal sounds. Little ones love it, perhaps because they find some of the animal sounds easier to imitate than most words.

Work with one stuffed animal at a time, not introducing more than three during the same activity period. For instance, take a stuffed dog in your hand and show it to your child. Then say, "This is a puppy. The puppy says, "woof-woof!" Ask your child, "Can you say woof-woof?" Reinforce any attempt he makes to repeat the correct sound by saying, "Yes, the puppy says woof-woof." If he says nothing or something totally different, simply repeat, "The puppy says woof-woof." In either case, encourage your child to repeat the animal sound again, perhaps prompting him with, "What does the puppy say?" If your child is able to follow along, repeat the same procedure with one or two other stuffed animals. Once your child can do this, be sure to try the "Old McDonald's Farm with Puppets" activity listed in the "Music and Movement" section of this book. Once he has mastered it, try pointing to pictures of the animals instead of holding a stuffed one.

Matching Animals with Their Pictures

Materials

- Stuffed animals
- Pictures of the same stuffed animals

Activity

Beginning to associate representations, such as pictures, with the real objects helps your child think in ways which will be necessary for him to think when he begins to write.

Set out two stuffed animals and one picture of each. Show your child one of the pictures and ask, "Which one does this look like? Does it look like puppy? (pointing to puppy) Or does it look like kitty?" (pointing to kitty) If your child is in the mood for this game, he will either point to or say the name of the correct animal. If he does so correctly, then reinforce it by saying, "Yes, that looks like the _____." If he does not answer correctly, say, "That looks like the _____" while pointing to the correct animal.

Once your child has mastered this activity with two stuffed animals, use a different set of two animals and their pictures and then another set.

Only after your child is comfortable playing this game with a variety of animals should you use more than two at a time, and even then more than three at a time would probably be too frustrating at this age.

Naming Stuffed Animals

Activity

Materials

• Stuffed
  animals

Begin with one realistic looking stuffed animal. For instance, say to your child, "This is a puppy." Then, if she is not speaking yet, say, "Touch or pet the puppy," as you help her do so. If she is already somewhat verbal, ask her to say "puppy." Reinforce any attempt she makes to repeat the naming word by saying, "Yes this is a puppy." If this is successful, do the same with one or two other stuffed animals.

Once your child can identify a few stuffed animals, then move on to the next stage of this activity by having her touch the specific animal you name while two animals are present. If your child is verbal, point to or touch one of the animals and ask, "What is this?" If your child is not yet verbal, say, "Touch the puppy." If she attempts to say the correct name or touches the correct animal, reinforce the answer by saying, "Yes, this is the puppy." If she does not answer or answers incorrectly, simply say, "This is the puppy."

Once your child can identify a few animals in either stage of this activity, introduce a few more. Then, try using pictures of animals instead of the actual stuffed animals.

Keep in mind that while these activities use animals as the theme, they can be done with any group of things—toys, fruits, vegetables, clothes, etc. They serve as patterns for teaching vocabulary, not just for teaching about animals.

Reading Books I Made

Materials

- Homemade books (See page 10.)

Activity

Reading books that your one-year-old has made helps develop her self-esteem by showing her that these books are valued and used just as much as other books.

Using the picture books, shape books, or the family album your child has already made, sit down next to her or hold her in your lap. Help her turn the pages and name the people or objects on each page. For example, if the first page of the family album has a picture of Grandma, point to the picture and say, "This is a picture of Grandma. Can you say Grandma?" Reinforce any attempt to answer correctly by saying, "Yes, this is Grandma." If she cannot answer correctly, simply say again, "This is Grandma." In either case, say again, "Who is it?" Then, let your child answer or answer for her if she does not. Move on to the next page and picture, following the same steps. Using this procedure, read through all the books you made together. Of course, how much you read at one sitting will depend on your child's attention span.

Mirror Talk

Materials

• Large mirror

Activity

For this activity you will make specific sounds while facing the mirror so that your child, who should also be looking at the mirror, can watch your reflection as he listens to your sounds. Sit with your child with the mirror in front of both of you. Make sounds with a slightly exaggerated facial expression. For example, say, "Ahh," over and over with your mouth open wide and then encourage your child to make that same sound. Try making each sound listed below for about one minute until you find one or two that your child can imitate. After he imitates one sound a couple of times, help him notice his face in the mirror the next time he makes that sound.

Over time your child will be able to imitate more and more sounds, so try making a variety of sounds each time you do this activity.

Suggested sounds:

◆ Ahh

◆ Ooh

◆ Ew

◆ Ha-Ha

Also try pursing your lips and making kisses in the mirror.

This Little Piggy

Materials

• Rhyme (See below.)

Activity

As you perform the words and actions listed below, encourage your child to join in, especially on repeating the last word of each line.

This activity is best done when your child is in a relaxed, happy mood. It is great to include as part of a massage.

This Little Piggy

The first little piggy went to market.

(Say this while tapping your child's big toe with your finger.)

The second little piggy stayed home.

(Say this while tapping your child's second toe.)

The third little piggy had _____ (Name a food your child likes.) (Say this while tapping your child's middle toe.)

The fourth little piggy had _____ (Name another food your child likes.) (Say this while tapping your child's fourth toe.)

The fifth little piggy cried, "Wee, wee, wee, wee" all the way home.

(Say this while tapping your child's little toe.)

High Chair Words

Materials

- Cup
- Spoon

Activity

Sit down with your child and place a spoon and a cup in front of both of you. (Be sure to use a spoon and cup that your child uses on a regular basis.) Hand your child the spoon and say, "This is a spoon. Can you say spoon?" Reinforce any attempt to say "spoon" by saying, "Yes this is a spoon." If your child does not try to say spoon, go ahead and repeat, "This is a spoon," and encourage him to try to say "spoon." If he doesn't try to say it after a few times, move on to the rest of this activity.

Next, hand your child the cup and follow the same procedure as you did for the spoon. If you still have your child's attention, move on to the next step.

Place the spoon and cup in front of both of you and point to or pick up the spoon, saying, "This is a spoon. What is it?" If your child does not respond, repeat, "This is a spoon." If he tries to say "spoon," say, "Yes, it is a spoon." Follow this same procedure with the cup and then with both objects in front of you, ask your child, "Show me the spoon. If he does so, say, "Yes, that is a spoon." If he cannot do so, you should point to the spoon and say, "This is a spoon." Follow this same procedure with the cup. Then switch back and forth a few times.

Puppet Show

Materials

- Puppets
- Large sheet of paper
- Pieces of tape

Activity

Have your child sit on one side of a doorway while you sit on the other side. Tape a large sheet of paper (the classified section of a newspaper will work fine) across the opening of the doorway to make a curtain/stage for your puppet show. The first puppet show you perform for your child should be the retelling of a story with which your child is familiar.

Later, you can introduce new stories with different puppets.

As your child grows older, she will enjoy putting on puppet shows for you. Be sure to encourage her early attempts at this.

My House

Materials

- None

Activity

Begin by showing your child some lights in your house. Point each one out and say, "This is a light." Then take your child into different rooms and say, "Show me a light," or "Do you see a light?" Say to your child, "Yes, that's a light" when she points to one. If she cannot point one out herself, then point it out and say, "Here's the light." If your child is verbal, encourage her to repeat the word "light" whenever you or she points one out. Praise any effort to repeat the word "light." Follow this procedure to help your child identify doors and windows in your house, too.

Name That Fruit

Materials

- Apple
- Banana

Activity

Sit with your child with one apple and one banana centered in front of both of you. Pick up the apple and say, "This is an apple. Can you say apple?" If she doesn't say it, you should repeat, "It is an apple" and encourage her to say apple. Then, ask your child to show you the apple. If she does so, say, "Yes that is the apple." If she can't say it or guesses wrong, point to the apple and say, "This is the apple." Do the same with the banana. Switch back and forth, asking about each fruit a few times.

Gradually introduce new fruits through this activity by keeping one of the previous fruits and adding new ones, one at a time.

Hear Me Talk!

Materials

- Tape recorder
- Tape cassette

Activity

Your child will love listening to himself talk. What better way to encourage his talking and listening skills than to tape record him. Simply begin talking to your child after you have set up the recording equipment, or surprise him by recording his conversations without him knowing.

After you have taped him, allow him to listen. At first he may be confused when you start playing the tape, but soon he will revel in the idea of hearing himself sing and talk.

You may want to consider buying a child-sized tape recorder for this activity(there are many on the market) so that your chid can carry the recorder with him and learn to play and record for himself.

Also, be sure to date your child's recorded masterpieces if you choose to save them. You may want to designate one tape for this purpose and tape once a month to document his language development. He'll love listening to it when he is older, too.

The World of Make-Believe

Introduction

The world of make-believe. Wow! The ability of humans to conceive of that which is not yet and which may never be part of reality is the world of the imagination—the world of make-believe! If you have forgotten about this fascinating world, let your child take you back as you play together through the activities in this section.

The following ideas capitalize on your one-year-old's love of imitative play. Let these activities be a beginning point for sparking other imaginative play of your own or your child's invention as she learns to navigate the world of make-believe. Developing the world of the imagination helps your child develop the ability to think abstractly—a skill necessary for many future endeavors in the intellectual, social, and purely creative areas.

Hat Dress-Up

Materials

- Variety of hats
- Mirror

Activity

Help your child try on hats of various sizes. Show him his reflection in the mirror with each of the different hats.

This is a good opportunity for your child to see that he is still himself even when external changes occur. To reinforce this concept, each time your child looks in the mirror with a different hat, say, "Look at _____ (child's name) in a _____." (Example: baseball cap, bonnet, etc.)

Laundry Derby

Materials

- Laundry basket
- Towels

Activity

Place a couple of clean towels in the bottom of the laundry basket and put your child inside it. Get her to sit down and then get behind the basket and push it. If you make some race car noises like "Zoom, Zoom!" while you push, this will add to the fun.

When you get tired of pushing the basket, help your child put one of her favorite stuffed animals or dolls in the basket and encourage her to push the basket around as you did, while making the race car noises, of course.

Remember, children this age love to climb onto and into things, so once you have introduced this activity, be sure not to leave your laundry basket any place where your child might injure herself by trying to climb in it.

Walking the Dog

Materials

- Large stuffed dog
- Collar
- Leash

Activity

Put a real collar and leash on your child's stuffed toy dog and show him how to pull it along with him as he walks. Encourage him to follow your example. Teach him to say things like "Here, boy" to the dog while he "walks" it.

If you have a real dog, be sure to make it clear to your child that he walks only his toy dog and only big people like Mommy, Daddy, or big sister/brother walk the real dog. Try having your little one walk his toy dog alongside you while you walk the real dog.

Bathing the Baby

Materials

- Baby bathtub
- Wash cloth
- Small towel
- Baby doll
- Water (optional)

Activity

First of all, if you want to use water, this activity is best done outside. Otherwise, set the tub on a child-sized table, put in the baby doll and pretend to start bathing it with the washcloth. After a little while, take the baby out of the "water" and "dry" it. Then help and encourage your child to repeat the entire process.

Safety Note: Never leave your child unattended with water. Even a very shallow amount is hazardous to a small child.

Tea Party

Materials

- Small plastic cups
- Pitcher

Activity

Set two cups and the pitcher on the floor or at a child-sized table and then sit down with your child and pretend to pour from the pitcher into both of your cups. Pretend to drink from your cup and exclaim in a playful voice, "This is good _____." (example: tea, juice, milk) If your child looks very confused, show her that there is nothing in your cup. Then, exclaim again about your drink. If she is ready for this activity, she will soon pick up her cup and pretend to drink, too. If not, try again in a month or so. If your child is able to play along, encourage her to pour some pretend drink from the pitcher and then ask her what she is drinking by saying something like, "Is that juice or milk?"

The next time you play "Tea Party," you might want to add some small plastic plates and pretend to eat something, as well.

Turtle Time

Materials

• Large basket

Activity

Demonstrate for your child and then help her to crawl around with the large basket on her back. Tell your child that there are animals that look like this and that they are called turtles. Show your child a real turtle if possible; if not, show her a picture of a turtle.

You will probably look quite humorous when you demonstrate this activity, so encourage your child to laugh with you by saying something like, "Mommy looks silly, doesn't she?"

Cup and String Telephone

Materials

• 2 plastic cups

• 1 string (about 5 feet long)

Activity

An adult should cut a piece of string about 5 feet long and punch a hole in the end of each plastic (disposable) cup. Then, tell your child you are going to play telephone. Show him how to put the cup to his mouth to talk and to his ear to listen. Begin by saying, "Ring, ring" and then help him to have a conversation with you.

This activity works best if your child is already talking some, but go ahead and try it even if he is in the "nonsense" jabbering stage.

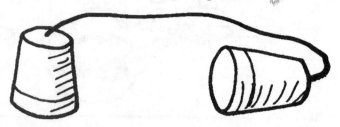

Little Driver

Materials

• One pot lid

Activity

Have your child sit on a rug or carpeted surface and then set the pot lid in front of him. Demonstrate how to hold the edges of the pot lid and move it like a steering wheel. Also, encourage your child to use the pot lid's handle for a horn and make "beep, beep" sounds while demonstrating this part of the activity. Once he is verbal, ask your child where he is going. If this confuses him, be more specific and ask, "Are you driving to Grandma's?" or "Are you driving to the store?"

Full Dress-Up

Materials

• Old clothes
• Old scarves
• Old shoes
• Old hats
• Mirror

Activity

Help your child put on some dress-up clothes and then let her look in the mirror. Encourage her to try different outfits and combinations of shoes, hats, and clothes. Then have her look at herself in the mirror each time. Playing dress-up helps your child begin to try out different roles.

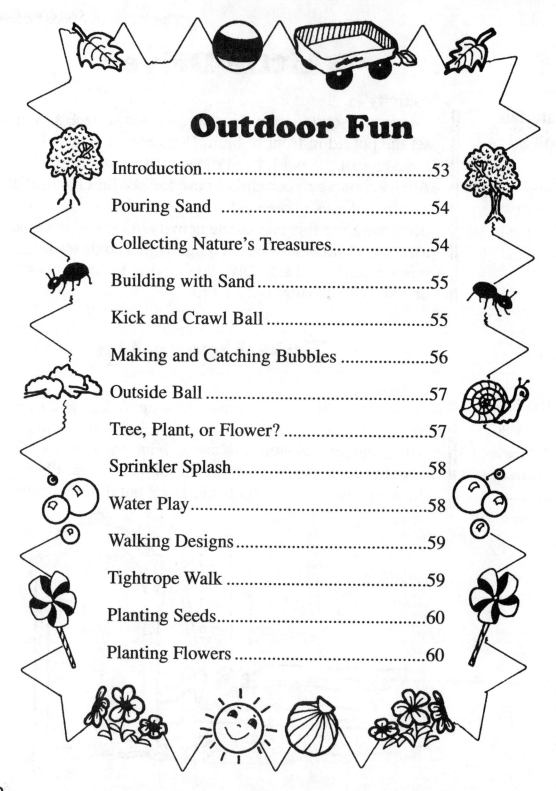

Outdoor Fun

Introduction

Children have always loved playing outside. They probably always will.
Not only are the fresh air and sunshine beneficial to your child's health and
well being, but the great outdoors offers a whole new world of experiences
and opportunities as your child's senses are invigorated, his mind stimulated,
and his body challenged.

Learning to respect plants, animals, and other natural wonders at an early
age leads to a lifetime of peaceful coexistence with nature, just as learning to
enjoy life both indoors and out leads to an active, well-rounded lifestyle.
The activities in this section will help develop your one-year-old's mind and
body as he learns and plays in one of his favorite spots. (**Note:** Be sure to
use sunscreen.)

Pouring Sand

Activity

Materials

- Sandbox
- Pitcher

This activity works best with dry sand. It should be done on a day that is not too windy in order to prevent sand from getting into anyone's eyes.

Show your child how to scoop up a pitcher full of sand and then how to slowly pour (not dump) it out. Demonstrate a couple of times and then hand the pitcher to her and encourage her to follow your scooping and pouring example. Initially, she may dump the sand rather than pour it—that is fine at this age. In either case, encourage your child to do this activity over and over, completely filling and emptying each time.

Collecting Nature's Treasures

Activity

Materials

- One bag or bucket
- Outdoor area

Tell your child that you are going to take a special kind of walk together. Tell him what you will be looking for to put into the bucket or bag on your walk. Find examples of what you will be collecting and put a few items into the container. Depending upon your child's level of coordination, it may be best for you to hold the bucket or bag while he concentrates on picking up the desired objects and placing them inside. However, if your child wishes to do all of the work, oblige. His quest for independence is much more important than making sure each item stays inside the container.

Building with Sand

Materials

- Unbreakable containers
- Sandbox with damp sand

Activity

Demonstrate for your child how to scoop up sand in a container so that the container is full. Then, show him how to pack the sand with his palm and level it off by swiping your palm across the open end of the container. Next, show him how to turn the container over on top of the rest of the sand in the sandbox. Do the same with another container or two as your child watches and then help him do what you have just demonstrated.

Note that this sand activity uses damp sand. If your sand is very dry, add a little water to the top layer in the sandbox. Also, remember that your child may wish to do his own thing with the sand. Do not be insulted if he just wants to play in it.

Kick and Crawl Ball

Materials

- One medium-sized, soft play ball (air filled is best)

Activity

When your child is quite steady on her feet, demonstrate how to stand directly in front of and kick a ball. Then, crawl, walk, or run to it. From that point, kick it again; then crawl, walk, or run to it and kick it again, etc. Have your child follow along while you move through your demonstration and then help and encourage her to follow the same procedure. As an alternative, play inside the house with a sponge (Nerf®) ball.

Remember, kicking a ball will most likely be a difficult task for your child. Give encouragement but be willing to give up the activity if your child is frustrated by it.

Making and Catching Bubbles

Materials

- Bubbles
- Bubble wand
- Unbreakable container

Activity

It is best to do this activity on dirt or concrete, as the bursting bubbles tend to make grass or a wooden deck slippery. Also, one-year-olds generally have not mastered blowing air out as opposed to sucking it in; therefore, note that the procedure suggested for making bubbles does not involve the mouth.

Purchase commercially prepared bubbles or make your own, using the recipe below. Demonstrate how to dip the bubble wand into the container holding the liquid. Next, wave your arm quickly, until the air makes bubbles blow out. Show your child how to chase and pop the bubbles. Demonstrate the whole procedure a couple of times and then help your child make the bubbles. Join in the fun as he chases and pops the bubbles. Encourage him to do the bubble making, chasing, and popping over and over again.

If your child enjoys chasing and popping the bubbles but cannot make them, you can make them while he catches and pops them for awhile.

Homemade Bubble Blowing Liquid

- 1 quart of water
- 4 tablespoons of glycerin
- 8 teaspoons of tincture of green soap (available at pharmacies)

Stir all ingredients together and store in a tightly covered plastic container.

Outside Ball

Materials

- One ball

Activity

Outdoors, in a large area , demonstrate to your child how to throw a ball. Be sure to use a ball small enough for your child to hold in one hand. Introduce the word "throw." Underhand throwing should be tried first, as it is easier for most children to master at this age—it is also a logical extension of rolling the ball.

Once your child has mastered underhand throwing, demonstrate overhand throwing. (Do not expect to do this on the same day as underhand throwing!) Each time you throw the ball, show your child that running to retrieve it is part of the fun.

It is good to use two different balls for "Inside Ball" and "Outside Ball" to help your child learn that we roll balls inside and throw them outside.

Tree, Plant, or Flower?

Materials

- Outdoor area containing trees, plants, and flowers
- Stroller (optional)

Activity

Take a walk with your child in an outdoor area which includes trees, nonflowering plants, and flowers. Pause at every, or most, trees, plants, and flowers, each time telling your child, "This is a _____." Encourage your child to repeat the word you have given. Reinforce your child's response or attempted response by saying, "Yes, this is a _____," using the word again. Then, continue your walk, pausing at the next tree, plant, or flower and repeating the above procedure.

Sprinkler Splash

Activity

Materials

- Sprinklers
- Water
- Towel

Children of all ages love to play in the sprinklers. Take advantage of a hot day and cool off in the sprinklers. Or, simply give your child the hose and turn it on low. Both you and your child can enjoy running around, getting wet, and having fun.

Be sure to use sunscreen, and choose a safe area such as the grass so that your child will not slip when the ground becomes wet. With any luck, a rainbow will appear and your child will delight in another outdoor beauty.

Water Play

Activity

Materials

- Water
- Food coloring
- Wash tub
- Sponge
- Squeeze bottle
- Cups and bowls

Fill your child's infant bathtub or another plastic container with water and mix in some food coloring. Place the tub at his level, for instance on a small table or chair, so that he can stand while experimenting with the water. Then give him a sponge, squeeze bottle (the kind that is sold with children's juice is perfect), and various small cups and bowls.

Show your child how to fill the cups and pour them out, how to transfer the colored water from one cup to another, how the sponge absorbs and can be squeezed, and how the bottle is filled and squirted out.

Most children love exploring with the many things they can do with water. Just emphasize the need to be careful when using water with one-year-olds.

Walking Designs

Materials

- Sidewalk chalk

Activity

Using thick sidewalk chalk, make the following types of lines for your child to walk on—wavy lines, large circles, zigzags, and large squares. Make the lines in this order, being sure that your child has mastered walking on one before moving on, as these are listed in order of difficulty. Also, be sure that you make the lines very thick. You should hold your child's hand and help her follow the lines the first few times you do this activity. Do not expect perfection, as a one-year-old does not have the coordination to follow these patterns exactly.

Tightrope Walk

Materials

- Rope

Activity

Using a coated rope (so that it does not chafe your child's hand), tie the ends to two fixed objects in your yard so that the rope is taut and is suspended at your child's hand level. Begin with the rope tied at a distance of about five feet and gradually increase the distance/rope length as your child masters the shorter distances. Once you have the rope securely tied, demonstrate for your child how to hold the rope as you walk along and then hold one of your child's hands and have her hold the rope with the other hand as you help her walk along the length of the rope. After a few tightrope walks together, encourage her to do it without your hand, but do not insist. She will let you know when he feels ready for that.

Be sure to do this activity over a grassy area so that your child will not be injured in case she does stumble and fall while walking along.

Planting Seeds

Materials

- Corn seeds
- Empty aquarium
- Potting soil

Activity

Help your child fill the aquarium (or other clear container with a flat bottom and tall sides) with potting soil. Then, with a finger help him make 1/2 inch deep indentations in the soil next to the glass, approximately every three inches, along one side of the aquarium. Next, help him put a couple of seeds into each indentation. Then, help him pack about 1/2 inch more soil on top of the seeds. Help your child sprinkle the aquarium with enough water so that the top is moist. Set the aquarium in a sunny window (seeded side to the light) and help your child water it twice daily. Encourage your child to look closely at the side where he planted the seeds when he does the watering.

Planting Flowers

Materials

- 3 to 5 flower plugs
- Sturdy spoon

Activity

Use small, fast-growing flower plugs such as zinnias or marigolds which are ready for transplanting and are available at local nurseries. For each plant, help your child use a sturdy spoon to dig a hole just slightly larger than the plug of soil surrounding each plant. Set the plant in the hole and cover the area around the plant with the soil that was removed from the hole. When all plants are in the ground, help your child water them thoroughly but gently. Watering should be repeated daily, as should checking for new growth. Show your child a picture of how the flowers will look so she can look forward to seeing them bloom. Once they bloom, let your child decide when and if she wants to pick them.

60

Away from Home

Introduction

It often seems one of the biggest challenges in parenting a young child is keeping her happily occupied while away from home. This section introduces fun, constructive activities that can be done in two of the most difficult places to be a one-year-old or her parent—in the car and in a restaurant. As your child learns and participates in these activities, she is learning independence as she does them alongside you but without your undivided attention, as you are mainly concentrating on another activity such as driving. She also learns constructive, acceptable ways to pass the time in what could otherwise be a frustrating situation for both of you. Taking a little time to prepare and to teach your child these activities and participating in those requiring your participation will help make the times away from home more pleasant for everyone.

Snack Time

Materials

- Favorite snack

Activity

Never underestimate the power of food! Having a favorite snack while driving in the car or waiting for service can appease a bored or cranky one-year-old. Simply pack your child's treat and reveal it when needed. Some parents even suggest having the favorites for moments of need only.

However, be sure you have another adult in the car if you give your child something to eat while you are driving. One-year-olds need more supervision and assistance with eating than the driver can safely provide.

Shake, Rattle, and Roll

Materials

- Rattle
- Keys
- Noisy toy

Activity

Before leaving to go somewhere, pack a few items that make noise, such as your child's rattle or keys. Think creatively! Measuring spoons, a play instrument, and even a whistle are fun items to make noises with. Just be sure the sounds will be appropriate for where you are going.

When you arrive at the location and have to wait, place the toys in from of both of you and ask your child to play each one. Then have her shut her eyes and listen to you use one object to make a noise. Immediately put the object back down and encourage her to open her eyes and pick the object that made the noise. Your child is sure to enjoy the challenge of determining which toy you used to make each sound.

Family Sing-Along

Activity

Materials

• Words to songs (See below.)

As you sing each song, encourage your child to join in on the choruses or special sounds and actions. Repeat them many times when you introduce a new song.

Old MacDonald Had a Farm

(Example with a cow)

Old MacDonald had a farm, E-i-e-i-o.

And on that farm he had a cow, E-i-e-i-o.

With a moo, moo here, and a moo, moo there.

Here a moo, there a moo, everywhere a moo, moo.

Old MacDonald had a farm, E-i-e-i-o.

(Begin the song again, using a different animal.)

If You're Happy and You Know It

If you're happy and you know it clap your hands.

If you're happy and you know it clap your hands.

If you're happy and you know it, then your face will surely show it.

If you're happy and you know it clap your hands.

(Begin the song again, using the following verses.

In place of "clap your hands," sing "stomp your feet."

In place of "clap your hands," sing "touch your nose.")

Family Sing-Along *(cont.)*

The Wheels on the Car

(Sing to the tune of "The Wheels on the Bus.")

The wheels on the car go round and round, round and round, round and round. (When singing "round and round," roll bent forearms over each other, held in front of your body.)

The wheels on the car go round and round, all over town.

The wipers on the car go swish-swish-swish, swish-swish-swish, swish-swish-swish. (When singing "swish-swish-swish," hold both palms in front of you and twist your wrists back and forth.)

The wipers on the car go swish-swish-swish, all over town.

The windows on the car go up and down, up and down, up and down. (When singing, "up and down," move arms up and down, bending at the elbow.)

The windows on the car go up and down, all over town.

The horn on the car goes beep-beep-beep, beep-beep-beep, beep-beep-beep. (When singing, "beep-beep-beep," push one fist out in front of you and move it as if pushing on a horn.)

The horn on the car goes beep-beep-beep, all over town.

65

Restaurant Colors

Materials

- Small squares of colored paper (primary colors)
- Plastic bag

Activity

Take one colored square, show it to your child, and tell him what color it is. Then, show him an item of food or other item which is that same color. For example, take an orange-colored square, show it to your child, and say, "This is orange." Then, show him the carrots on a family member's plate and say, "These carrots are orange, just like this orange paper." Continue this procedure with other colors and foods or other items. This is a great game to play while waiting anywhere. Just be sure to take along a plastic bag of colored paper squares.

Matching Shapes

Materials

- Construction paper
- Small plastic bag

Activity

Before leaving home, an adult should cut out two circles from one color of paper, two squares from another color of paper, and two triangles from another color of paper. Place all the shapes in a plastic bag. This activity is also a great way to educate and entertain your child while waiting in many places. At a restaurant, for instance, take out two sets of two shapes and place them in front of you and your child. Pick up one and show it to your child. Ask her if she can find another one like it. Go ahead and use the color and shape words, even though they won't mean much to your child now. Help your child find the matching shapes the first few times and before long she will be doing it by herself. Once your child has mastered this activity using two sets of shapes, add the third set of shapes.

Cracker Drop

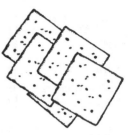

Materials

- Crackers or croutons
- Unbreakable cup or bowl

Activity

Waiting in a restaurant with a one-year-old can be a stressful experience. Use this activity and the following ones to engage your child and have a little fun while waiting.

Make a pile of crackers/croutons in front of your child and place the cup next to the stack. Demonstrate how to drop the crackers or croutons one by one into the cup and then how to take them back out one by one, putting them back into a stack. Encourage your child to repeat this activity many times, following the procedure you demonstrated of putting them all in and then taking them all out.

Object Peek-a-Boo

Materials

- Items from table
- Large napkin

Activity

Place one item such as a package of crackers, spoon, coaster, or sugar packet from the table in front of your child and then quickly cover it with the napkin. Wait a couple of seconds, uncover the item, and say, "Peek-a-boo!" Do this over and over, using different items.

As an alternative, you may also want to play this game as a version of "Magic Tube," listed under "Sensory-Motor Games." Using a toilet paper tube, as it is smaller and more portable than a paper towel tube, let your child enjoy making table items disappear and reappear. Keep an eye on your utensils, however. You will soon need them!

Puzzle Time

Materials

- Puzzle pieces
- Small bag

Activity

Before leaving the house, pack the pieces from a favorite puzzle in a small bag. When you are required to wait at the restaurant, pull out the bag and surprise your child. Even without the back board, your child will find delight in putting the puzzle together on the table. Talk about the puzzle's picture(s) and count the pieces with your child.

Play Dough Fun

Materials

- Play dough
- Table surface

Activity

Taking play dough along is easy and fun for the entire family. Everyone enjoys playing and making different shapes and creatures while waiting for a meal, especially one-year-olds. Simply pack a small amount of play dough in your purse or diaper bag and remove it when needed.

Be sure to see the play dough activity in the "Art Projects" section of this book for more ideas and the recipe for play dough.

Fun with Food

Introduction

The activities in this section will help meet your one-year-old's growing need for independence. By doing these activities, your child will feel a sense of accomplishment from creating things by herself. She will also enjoy the positive feedback from others who compliment her efforts. What a great way to build your child's budding self-esteem!

Bear in mind that a one-year-old is capable of doing more and more each day. Be sure to foster her growing need for independence and growing self-esteem by praising her efforts and sharing her glory in the end product, even if it doesn't look perfect to you. Remember that the goal of these activities is the process, rather than perfection of the product. Have fun and share your child's sense of wonder and amazement as she creates with food!

Tasting Party

Materials

- Muffin tin
- Assorted foods

Activity

Using a six-section muffin tin, place six different food samples in it (one per muffin cup). Be sure each food sample is distinctly different from the others. See the list of suggested foods below. Encourage your child to taste each food, giving the name of each as it is sampled. For example, you can say, "That is grapefruit, it tastes sour." It is good to vary the foods used in this activity as you change the focus from differing tastes to differing textures.

Note: Be sure to supervise this activity closely and to use foods that do not present a choking hazard.

Suggested foods:

- potato chips (use for salty, crunchy)
- grapefruit (use for sour)
- jello (use for sweet and squishy)
- dried apricots (use for sweet and chewy)
- pretzels (use for salty and crunchy)
- O-shaped unsweetened cereal (use for crunchy)
- mini-marshmallows (use for soft and sweet)
- sour pickles (use for sour and crisp)
- banana slices (use for sweet or slippery)

Gingerbread People

Materials

- Gingerbread people cookies
- Frosting
- Raisins

Activity

An adult should bake the cookies and allow them to cool. Just before you are ready to do this activity with your child, put two dots of frosting on the face (to show where the raisin eyes should go and to secure them), then put three dots of frosting down the body (to show where the raisin buttons go and to secure them). Once that is done, bring your child to the work space. Have a pile of raisins there and bring out one gingerbread person at a time, except for the first time when you demonstrate step by step on one while your child follows your actions. Say, "This is a gingerbread person. We are going to put eyes on it like this." Help your child follow your example and put eyes on his gingerbread person one at a time. Then, tell your child that you are going to give the gingerbread person some buttons. Help your child to put buttons on his gingerbread person. After demonstrating, help your child decorate the other gingerbread people the same way.

Circus Cookies

Materials

- Vanilla wafers
- Animal crackers
- Frosting

Activity

An adult should spread a very thick layer of frosting (at least a tablespoon) on the flat side of each vanilla wafer. Allow the frosting to set for at least 30 minutes and then show your child how to stand up an animal cracker in the frosting on each cookie. Talk about the names of the animals while you do this activity. Also, talk about the color and flavor of the frosting you are using. You can use any flavor of frosting, but your one-year-old will probably be more attracted to one that is colored.

Peanut Butter Worms

Materials

- Wax paper
- Recipe (See below.)

Activity

An adult should mix the ingredients according to the recipe below and then help your child roll out the "worms." To do this, have her work on a surface covered with wax paper. Washing her hands before working with food is a good habit to begin establishing now. Pinch off a bit of the dough (about a tablespoon) and demonstrate for your child how to put the dough on the wax paper and then move it back and forth with the palm of her hand until it is shaped like a worm. Help her keep it thick enough so it will stay together. After demonstrating the procedure, help and encourage your child to make as many peanut butter worms as she desires.

Peanut Butter Worms

- 1 cup peanut butter

- 1 cup honey

- 2 cups instant nonfat dry milk powder

- 2 cups instant oatmeal

Mix all ingredients thoroughly and then form the dough into "worms." Store at room temperature or refrigerate. Unused dough can be stored in the refrigerator for about two weeks.

73

Making Pizza

Materials

- English muffins
- Spaghetti or pizza sauce
- Grated cheddar cheese
- Grated mozzarella cheese

Activity

An adult should split the English muffins and lay them on a baking sheet. Then, spread spaghetti or pizza sauce on each one. As your child's coordination improves, he will enjoy helping with this step as well. Then, show your child how to sprinkle the cheese over the sauce. Encourage his efforts and don't worry about cheese spilling elsewhere on the baking sheet. As your child's taste buds mature, he will enjoy adding other toppings to his pizza. After your child has put the cheese and toppings on the pizzas, put them under the broiler for a minute or two. Be sure to allow them to cool adequately before allowing your child to eat one.

Coloring My Food

Materials

- Paper plate
- Crayons

Activity

An adult should draw some basic outlines on the paper plate to depict the shapes of the food that the child will be receiving. For example, draw a circle to represent a hamburger and some long, thin rectangles to represent French fries. Draw one item of food (for example, the circle/hamburger) first and say to your child, "This is a round circle like the hamburger you're going to eat. You can color it brown." Then, give your child a brown crayon and demonstrate how to color, if necessary.

When your child has finished coloring the first item, draw another food item she will be receiving (for example, the French fries), following the same procedure as you did for the hamburger. Do this for all the food items your child will be receiving.

Holiday Fruit Balls

Materials

- Recipe (See below.)

Activity

An adult should mix the ingredients according to the recipe below. Then, help your child make out the individual candies. If your child cannot yet roll the candy into balls, you can either have her make them into "worms," as in the "Peanut Butter Worms" activity listed earlier in this section, or you, the adult, can make the ball and then let your child flatten them into patties with her fist or palm.

Holiday Fruit Balls

- 1 cup toasted walnuts, chopped

- 2 cups dried apricots
- 2 cups dried cranberries

- 2 teaspoons orange juice
- 1 tablespoon light Karo syrup

Put walnuts in a food processor and process, using the metal blade, until they are very finely chopped. Add apricots and process them with the walnuts until they are very finely chopped and well blended. Add cranberries to the walnuts and apricots, and process until they are finely chopped and all are well blended. Transfer this mixture to a mixing bowl and add the orange juice and syrup, mixing until well blended. Pinch off a tablespoon at a time and roll into balls. Place these candy balls on a baking sheet or platter that has been lined with wax paper. Let the candy sit at room temperature for one day before serving it so that flavors can meld together. Holiday fruit balls can be stored at room temperature for up to ten days or in the freezer for up to one month.

Handy Cookies

Materials

- Slice 'n' bake cookies
- Cookie sheet

Activity

An adult should slice the cookies 1/2 inch thick each and place a few on a cool baking sheet. Try not to crowd the cookie sheet as this will make it difficult for your child. Take your child's hand with his palm flat and show him how to press his hand down hard on the dough (or demonstrate with your own hand). Encourage your child to put his hand print on each slice of cookie dough. Bake the cookies, cool them, and then show your child his handprint on each cookie. Allow him to eat one cookie right away and then help him show them off and share them with others.

Note: This activity affords a good opportunity to emphasize the safety rule that only grown-ups touch hot things.

JELL-O® Treats

Materials

- 4 packages of JELL-O®
- Large bowl
- 13 x 9-inch pan
- Cookie cutters
- Spatula

Activity

Follow the directions on any JELL-O® gelatin box to make the treats. You will need to do the first part of this activity without your child, as it involves boiling water and could pose a hazard to your child.

Once the JELL-O® is firm, give your child several cookie cutters, and show her how to press the shapes through the gelatin. Use a spatula to remove the shapes.

As an alternative, help your child use plastic eggs to reach into the cooled liquid mix and scoop the egg full. Place the eggs in the refrigerator and await colorful JELL-O® eggs!

Bibliography

Resources
These books provide wonderful information about one-year-olds. Try your local bookstore or library.

Ames, Ilg, & Haber. *Your One-Year-Old.* Dell Publishing Co., Inc., 1982.

Bavolek, Juliana. *Nurturing Book for Babies and Children.* Family Development Resources, Inc., 1989.

Dinkmeyer, Dinkmeyer, & McKay. *Parenting Young Children.* American Guidance Service, 1989.

Montessori, Maria. *The Absorbent Mind.* Dell Publishing Co., Inc., 1984.

Singer & Revson. *A Piaget Primer: How a Child Thinks.* Penguin Books, U.S.A., Inc., 1978.

Singer & Singer. *Partners in Play.* Harper & Row, 1977.

White, Burton. *The First Three Years of Life.* Avon Books, 1975.

Sources for Music
Bartels, Joanie. *Lullaby Magic.* BMG Music. No date.

Berstein's Favorites. (CD) *Children's Classics.* Sony, 1991.

Feinstein, Michael. (CD) *Pure Imagination.* Elektra, 1992.

Lewis, Shari. (CD) *Lambchop Sing-Along.* A & M, 1988.

Raffi. *Baby Beluga.* Troubadour Records, 1982.

Raffi. *Bananaphone.* Troubadour Records, 1994.

Raffi. *Rise and Shine.* Troubadour Records, 1982.

Sharon, Lois, and Bram. *The Elephant Show.* Drive Entertainment, 1994.

Bibliography

Books for One-Year-Olds
It is never too early to start instilling a love for reading! These books are excellent additions to your child's growing book collection.

Ahlberg, Janet, & Allan Ahlberg. *Peek a boo!* Puffin, 1981.

Brown, Margaret. *Goodnight Moon.* Harper & Row, 1947.

Freeman, Don. *Corduroy.* Viking Penguin, Inc., 1987.

Dr. Suess. *The Cat in the Hat.* Random House, 1957.

Frankel, Alona. *Once Upon a Potty.* Barron, 1984.

Hill, Eric. *Spot.* Puffin, 1988.

Johnson, John. *My First Book of Things.* Random House, 1979.

Kunhardt, Dorothy. *Pat the Bunny.* Simon & Schuster, 1967.

Martino, David. *Play-a-Sound Hey Diddle Diddle!* Publications International, Ltd., 1994.

Rey, Margret and H.A. *Curious George.* Houghton Mifflin Co., 1966.

Skaar, Grace. *What Do the Animals Say?* Scholastic Book Service, 1973.

Steiner, Charlotte. *My Slippers Are Red.* Knopf, 1957.

Wegman, William. *Triangle Square Circle.* Hyperion , 1995.

White, Stephen. *Barney's™ Favorite Nursery Rhymes: A Read Along Play-Along Book.* The Lyon's Group, 1993.

Wright, Blanche Fisher (illustrator). *Real Mother Goose.* Checkerboard.

Zelinsky, Paul O. (adapted by). *The Wheels on the Bus.* Dutton, 1990.